Here is a unique poetic voice. Acute obse
imagination make the everyday appear ex
collection. Thomas animates the world to
*prayer, perhaps, / that quivers like a globe of midges , philadelphus / makes
the path feel less alone".* The language is a heady blend of the
colloquial and reflective; humorous and elegiac. The imagery –
arresting, original and always, always alive.
—John Sewell

A Time for Such a Word is a collection that offers a new delight with
every turn of the page. The characters and landscape are brought to
life in a series of finely-crafted and thought-provoking poems, in
which memories and insight fuse with curiosity and fascination for
the world and its inhabitants. Vivid imagery and love of language
pulse through these poems. If you like Dylan Thomas, you will
love these. If you like Ted Hughes, you will love these. If you like
poetry, you will love these.

—Alison Chisholm, Poetry Columnist, *Writing Magazine.*

Michael W. Thomas' poems are rich with the details of past and
present lives. They explore the widest – and wildest – possibilities
of those lives with passion and humour.
—Alison Brackenbury

I really enjoy this book. There is much about the real world, past
and present. However, the work comes from the imagination with
a fine combination of rhythm, wordplay and image driving it
forward in a way that is unusual in the modern poetry world. You
have the impression of a constantly evolving tapestry. There is a
sense of mortality, notably in the fine poem for the Poet's father,
but there is also a sense of wonder and a reaching out to the stars:
*"[The boy] cannot believe / so much dying and birth / way up in the tall
silence."* Some of the images are wonderful: *"A prayer, perhaps, / that
quivers like a globe of midges."*
—Fred Beake, editor of *The Poet's Voice,* 1983-2000, author of *Out
of Silence* and *The Whiteness of Her Becoming.*

A Time for Such a Word

Michael W. Thomas

A Time for Such a Word

To Lynda
as Always

Seyton: The queen, my lord, is dead.
Macbeth: She should have died hereafter;
  There would have been a time for such a word.
    —Macbeth, Act V, scene v.

Contents

1. Each Hour has Held Him to its Needs

A Year to Speak

Each day I hide a word

on a post in an open field,
maybe, or where a kite's tail
snags unregarded
on a bush that's forgotten its summer

I have given myself a year to speak

or behind the bracket of a precinct light
in gaps between an electric parrot's options

a word a day
would be two sonnets
and the paunch of a third,
a pocket ode,
a round-the-houses lyric

sometimes furled in the hollow eye
of a statue of renown
sometimes in the heart of a first scream
or the motes that settle on a last

not that there'll be time
for style and polish
just as there's long been no world

an orator's cud is a safe place
so are the bossy repeats of an older twin

what I say
will depend on the order
in which I catch the words up,

on whether some few knot or spill
as I heap them to my mouth

love is the safest place of all—
people's vague afterthoughts,
guilted professions—
room enough there for my words to spread,
plenty of vaulted echo.

It might at year's end
be only a joke I offer
as I trail hands through such grasses as remain
or pause above a city's iron downs.

It might be something of remembrance
for those who slip round me
on their way to whatever
they think they may become
or to where their petals fold
as light unmakes,
whichever is the sooner.

A prayer, perhaps,
that quivers like a globe of midges.

Or nothing more
than one of the ways
that speak us as pain and footsteps,
as a sigh for any moment that relents,
as arms to open,
hands to interlace—

like well, there you have it
or we'd best get on
or lordy, lordy, here's another day.

A Boy Looks Out

It is evening. A boy looks out of his window.
His day has turned for home like all the others.
Each hour has held him to its needs
with grappling hands, then released him
to the next with its exact same tote
of scuffles and yells and dismay.

Now he is alone and unthreaded.
He could if he wished in a single breath
move and stay put. And so he does,
spreading his hands on the windowsill,
taking in the sky.

By now all the stars have lifted clear
of the pools and canals they shipped across
as time was seeing off the winter blue.
The boy looks from one to the next
and the next. He cannot believe
so much dying and birth
way up in the tall silence. He watches
as they peal their whiteness, hopes for a comet
to slice his drape-marshalled world.

He thinks about thinking. If his thoughts were stars
and he spilled them over the tedium of day,
people might say here's a tale
with no clue to its in or its out,
here are half-rhymes unmated
from a riddler caught between sea and shore,
dealing in thicks of mist.

The boy likes that. Likes the fancy
of puddling stars amongst the bony rectitude
of corridor and rule.
And now one star thwarts its form,
reshapes as a beckoning finger.
So the boy raises his. The million miles crimp.
The fingers touch. His unblemished soul
finds the words of ancient fire.

Uffern Gwaedlyd

Something made me look up
and there was my father
running out of the water at Swansea Bay
on Christmas Eve, aged nine,
yelling *uffern gwaedlyd, uffern gwaedlyd,*
till his mother, a waiting towel-matador,
cuffed his head with her elbow,
told him not to speak lowliness
what with Jesus on the way.
Further off, his father watched the others
haring up the shingle with worse on their lips,
pointed his stick at each in turn
like a Maesteg judge grading cattle
and cried *Jiw, Jiw, boys, that is quite enough.*
Then they were off
to a house built of washdays
and what was for them a slap-up meal
whose aromas broadened like magic webs
across the distempered ceiling.

I met my grandparents just a time or two
in rooms almost dark
but for anxious, prodding flames
that sketched their skin wizened
and pressed coal-black eyes deep into their heads.
I met my father a time or two as well
between his engagements with Arms and Crowns
and…the crimper, was it, on the side?
No, the chauffeuse. The crimper was long afterwards,
thickening the shadows beyond his final bed.

When free he would loom at the evening table,
ask me, *How was your day, lad, in all?*
like he was fresh in from the Spanish Main
and I'd been patient on a spit of cliff,
hopping from foot to foot,
hoisting a lamp to the stars.

Now, when I picture my father,
he looms just so as I'm sat small
but I see nothing of the chauffeuse-man,
only a nine-year old
uffern-ing up the beach
and, waiting with a tut, a tear,
towel wide as a muzzle-catch,
my mother.

Uffern gwaedlyd: (Welsh) Bloody hell.

*Jiw, Jiw: (Welsh) Good heavens! A softening of 'Duw' (God) to sound
less blasphemous. (With thanks to Sharon Larkin.)*

Deeper In, Further Off

I'll always remember that garden.
The branch-hands of the ornamental pear
scrabbling at high winter,
knocking each other out of the way
as if mad for the last bun on the plate.
The green feeder the wind could never budge,
next to the black one that twanged up and down
like a traffic light strung over Main Street
in a midwestern dust-blow in June.
The small summer-house
way back against the lane-wall
whose colours hardly stirred,
whose corners frittered into hornbeam and rose.

My parents did not desire my death
in fact. To err on the safe side, though,
I was of the garden as often as could be,
each time folding deeper in, further off,
till a lane-walker happening to pause at the gate
might have noticed the singular furl of a trunk,
the elbow crick of grey, the bushing of blue into sallow,
and sworn a spirit was broad across the day
then caught themself, laughed, maundered on.

Middle Ash

South Staffordshire

For seven years
we lived on the left side
of the only semis for miles.
The footings felt for the shoulder of a hill
like someone who knows he's drunk
and suspects that midnight steps are icy.
Inter-war brick, they were,
with a sort of bonemeal cladding.
Still, a trick of elevation
kept us clear of squire's sight-lines
and spared us parish disdain.

Buses to anywhere were twice a day
so if you missed them
the world hitched its skirts and didn't know you.
Mornings were a punch to the eye
from the deserts of rape below.
At weekends my brother and I
would trek to the airport at Halfpenny Green,
soak up what we felt it must be like
to take off with people you didn't know
and have crowds all over you
wherever you touched down.
Stuff this, he said, one August day
and got a job in a place where
you could throw a stone from the window
and hit a publican, doctor or cop
without even meaning to try.

The old man next door
dropped where he stood

between his apples and the courtesy box
he kept for his hens' fitful yield.
There was talk of a business conversion—
ponytails swarmed all over his side
the whole of a week near one Christmas
and made kissy-love to their phones.
But in the end it was boarded up—rats got in,
pigeons cooed their last down the chimney.
I started to feel like our life
had a corpse on its back.
Each time Dad phoned the council
they responded by burying their offices
deeper under Bridgnorth.
It got so a walk down the Bobbington Road
was a proper pied-piper affair,
all the ghosts of neglect and forgetfulness
mopping and mowing at my heels—
till the last time I walked it
and caught a miraculous bus
to where folks didn't only trip over your name
when the census erupted
or the rates fell due.
Mum and Dad stayed on,
ossified between modern-method farms
and weekend homes
with solar panels like outsize covers
of etiquette guides for God.

Yesterday
I caught a programme
where a row of minster faces
sang yearningly of the country year
and maidens who live on yonder hill
among the leaves so green. O.
I'd only just bought the set

9

or I might have surrendered
to the whisper of my fist.

What happened
to the ashes either side
I'll never know.

Slow to Clear

There's one light out there.
The fog isn't yet what it may be.
Twice I lift and let fall my hand
pretending to sketch the pillared folds
of the curtains dropping clean
either side of the window.
I turn my head.
The room nudges up
its all but colourless angles.
It is dawn. It is morning.
It is no time. On the wall
is a painting of a boat
run up on nowhere sands
perhaps Rosslare
or granite Brittany.
Around the light switch
the plate snags a fugitive gleam
like the lees of all riches.
I hear whistling cut from a body
in the murk. I hear the grizzle of motion
as an engine crests and sinks
below itself. The fog thickens.
The one light disappears. On the path
a cat stalks a single fetch of shadow
in hope that it has enough give.
It steps in and never was.
And now a single cry far out on that sea
could be the very world
unfastening its soul
rocking against the effort
then for all time still.

Shortest Days

I can see why,
at this time of year,
some might be tempted
to book alone into a hotel—
an edge-of-town place, say,
with a view of sleeping fields,
unpestered by the low-level riot
of shopping fed to the boots of cars
or tinsel-brass funnelled
down thronging narrows.

I can picture them
(having booked in and said, no, that's fine,
they can manage their bags)
sitting on the edge of the bed,
maybe catching brief sight
of the faux-wooden mini-bar,
maybe wondering if the wardrobe
has proper hangers
or the type you have to faff
on and off those little hooks;
maybe wondering if they should have brought
that extra bottle after all.

Then turning to look at those fields
with their rough exultation of hedges,
their birds at this and that twig,
dipping and twisting for a pick of winter food.
Maybe inhaling the pot-pourri'd air,
spreading a hand on the counterpane,
to feel the old year pulse along their arm
and out at their fingers' ends.

And thinking of the new year
already stirring its stumps—
imagining the face it will turn to them
out of all the coming months. Hoping
that at least it can manage a come-and-go smile,
that it won't simply be a gaze uninflected
as from someone who has fumbled their heart
and cannot feel, cannot act
except in leaden ways—
who vaguely remembers
that there was something like love
but now, for the life of them,
cannot place what it moved, how it meant,
what in all their silenced world
it might once have been for.

That Lane Gone By

Where is safest to live after all?
Down that lane gone by in a flash,
perhaps, the kind that sires a blind twist
or two, that shoots long drives
to houses that must have built themselves
when summer wasn't looking—
then gives up and folds under tipsy fences
and rising splashes of grass.

Or round the back
of that lipless jug on the garden-room sill,
set down and forgotten
on the way from kitchen to tip,
that turns a blue escutcheon
to the uncaring day
and suffers heat and cold
to go halves in worming its glaze.

Or in the moment
when you can no longer hear
a pleading voice and a car
tearing off in low gear
or the tears of a child
who's been told they have to go
or can never come back

or after the final words
of someone you always thought you knew
but who in an instant
has laid off humanity
like a coat of shovel-armed fit
and is now a stranger
a work of ice

and dashes away all you meant to them
as though it was so many cluster-flies
where fruit outruns its season
and must sink
into its slow disfashioning.

Thursdays

The Welsh Marches

I drive on a road in mountain country
in almost early evening
on the Thursday of my life.
Road signs play tag with two nations,
grasses lie low on the verge.
Here's a man leaning on something overgrown
who pokes his head out
from whatever the day has served him
and raises his hand to greet me
or say, just you drive on. Further,
two walkers are thrashing at their map,
shrugging, turning it over
as if to mottle their boot-caps with its runes
and start or end with nothing only white.

Thursdays have been richly in my life.
Took the last of a holiday with them
as it funnelled into nothing
from the car's back window
when all that lay ahead
were months of unlovely brickwork
and light that barely roused.
Doled out the moments
as I traded hard words
and a marriage turned to graffiti.
At times did nothing more than fill up
with sleet by noon,
particoloured anger,
the cavern-drips of regret...

…but as often spilled a prodigious sky
for me to gaze up at
from the unenchanted ruck,
shaped joy out of bits and ends
as a dome coaxes match-light—

as right now,
with the road signs swapping tongues,
the tyres firm, the sky middling bright,
and me with an eye
on what could be a black hill
or simply a grievance of the clouds,
knowing I can't know how far it is away
so deciding to slow a bit, wind down the window,
give my elbow its ease
and marvel at the artwork of a 'Pick Your Own' board
that rears without hurry
where a gate must once have been.

Around the Roads Round

Let's go all around the roads round.
The day may well be waiting to crowd us
with its pitted watchman's face
and at its back the rattle of all its drums.
Or we may be lucky to happen upon
a forest of trees all spindled and wide apart
and watch as the last leaf falls from each
the next and the next wherever we look
as if compelled by orderliness
and the unfussed exits from life.
Let's dig deep beyond the town
with our eyes blanking its lights.
That way we might dodge infection
from how all has been boned and strung
and make a place that folds easy
against how we wish to live.
Even the rain and snow might fall
more solicitously, even the sun
might look to its rise and set
with more than the usual coarseness.
Let's find a hill. Let's walk on the spot
at the entrance to an unconsidered lane.
Let's turn the hours like a card carousel
to be absently fingered. Let's draw breath slowly
as though to taste the full of the world
then breathe out as if we were pocket gods
in the margins of old cartography
inventing north-east and south-south-west
with every blow of engraved apple cheeks
and flipping grass underside upside
disarraying the crests of morning birds
for the pleasure of seeing them settle again
for the pleasure of warming at their shine.

Cannula Loops

Now I am only a diffident breath.
Sometimes it is enough
to float me over the minutes,
at others it just stutters me through
so time comes cold around me
as a wave shrouds a bared head.

Once I was more: in a pub, say,
at the top of the town,
my hand would steady the opening glass
till Friday night turned nut-brown
at the back of my throat. My eyes
would laugh loud as a friend's
as he fizzed with more joy
than could be delivered
before the cloths went on.

And further back, along school corridors
when afternoon was done,
I would dance a fool's jig,
dishevel the hair of ghostly teachers
lost in how their bodied selves
had moved through the emptying day,
minds full of tears and soured wonder,
commuter stare coursing the run of the tiles.

So long ago. I could not have foretold
how over time, by inches,
a throw disappoints a stone,
a stretch folds into drumming fingers,
best foot forward is reveille
for hearts yet to beat.

I could not have known,
in the paradisal jolt
of the first dive of summer,
that I would become
a praiser of handrails,
disciple of the fen,
drifter on a shoreline
where the winds rise and fall
in adjustable trebles—

that I would be a house
uncertain whether to stand as joisted
or veil its plot
in the mist of ruination.

From this Day

What will I take from this day
but a pigeon's coo stuck in the chimney
when the bird itself is in stumbling flight
to the next mile of the dusk.
What will I hear from this day
but the words *Goodbye…sorry*
balanced on a withdrawing hand
and, moments later,
carriage doors rushing to meet,
the tracks' waning mither,
a platform left to absorb itself
in the safety line's yellow jog.
What will I see from this day
but the man who collides
at the turn to my crescent,
drunk as elevenpence,
flinging all he's ever been
in staggers to right and left.
Sorry again—meant for me
or the wife he'll have to face
by the bulb of a somewhere kitchen
or perhaps himself
for all the mischances he piloted,
all the *yeses* he signed up to
without even moving his lips
and how each pitched him
one scuttle further from himself,
so that now he barely knows who it is
who chafes his way over kerbs and Mondays
with a foxed map in his head
from which *home* is carelessly leaching.

Sins Beyond its Making

Now and again
I turn my clocks to the wall
so their thrum
can dwindle as it will
down the paintwork,
across the day's occlusions.

Time needs its rest too,
needs to cry silently
in its place of no depth or echo.

It is called on endlessly
to be the potboy of momentousness,
to have age and epoch
tied to its leg
as a tin can might hunt a dog
through thorn and waste.

Forever it must feel
the grit of late and early
pressed deep into its skin
as though it were invented
expressly to be blamed.

Time takes hit after hit
for sins beyond its making.
Which is why it needs
ever and again
to sit with its bedevilments,
to sob in wonder
at why it ever was,
to face itself as a question alone
much as an ancient fingerpost
might accept it points to nothing now
and knows no way.

Out of a Box

Last week
in a public garden,
I took all my yesterdays
out of a box
and twined them round the summer.
I'd brought an armload of signs
to show the different prices
but abandoned all that
when I saw the shine
in the eyes of the people
who came in dribs and twitches
then thickened with the morning
where ball games were not.

Some of them eased a particular day
from between the petals
but wrinkled their noses and stuffed it back.
Others stared disbelieving at their choice
as though it were one of their own long-agos
and I had broken and entered.
Gingerly they replaced it, pressing down
as you might try to hold a ghost's head under water.

Lads riffled through my childhood
eager for a time that made no sense—
village elders, runic jokes,
how to freight a yellow-eyed cat with curses.
A pleasant person read over and over
the moment when I knew the world
was at least a shoe-size bigger than mine,
then let it drop in a leaf-swirl
to the hands of (I guess) her grand-daughter.

But most in the end were taken
by a man of triangular stance,
who'd been fobbed off, he said,
with suet and scrub
and so had omitted to live.
Slowly he opened the skin round his heart
and slotted in my histories
like letter-tiles that at last cheat nonsense.

I watched him go as the gates began to close,
saw how he quivered from my car-crash loves,
expanded round the final moment
of that last-ever exam,
round afternoons alone on high hills
or lost in sunspots playing tag on harbour waters—
as he stilled into the minute I'd set down my box
and started to blemish the day.

There was one last paring of time.
I'd placed it where no-one could see.
Now, as the first of dark
spidered the trees,
I retrieved and read it
and did as I was told.

Last and Closest

My last and closest friend
is a flake of white paint.

It looks like a tear at the full,
the kind that might start
when memory gets to its clawed feet
or afternoons give up on sunlessness.

It must have survived a refit
somewhere in the mists of the house,
must have stuck to a jumper,
hung in the dark like a cancelled star,
ridden at my waist
as I tried to match stair to heartbeat
or some errand forced me out
among the ashen places—

till I saw it,
heard how it cried itself over and over,
took and laid it
on a swatch of evening blue,
watched how it gathered and spent itself
like truths insisting.

Now we're inseparable.
I find myself hosting unobligated smiles,
a laughter that was never before
teased from me.
I tell it all my life:
what got me out of my April beds,
how my summers kept something of dignity
when nothing only echo
answered their calls.

My flake of paint listens
snug in my palm or the deeps of a pocket.
I hear it understand.

Some days we coast
through the pools of unchanging people.
Others we let the phone ring on
while someone I knew
stays as elsewhere as ever.
Always we watch
as the world rolls widdershins from the sun
and the moon comes in
with its knockings of wax or wane.

Always then my friend asks the question.
Always I say, never fear—
brighter, you are, and truer
than the pair of them at their damndest.

That Time

Because sometimes it steals upon you
when you're looking in the window of a shop
or find you have ten minutes extra
to cool your heels before whatever it is
that might pizzazz the hour.

Strange to think it could be early morning—
that of a sudden, as the sounds of the first cars
wash across the walls, as the radio
bloats with worldly fecklessness,
you might be not there.

The day will maunder on,
dispensing the blitz of first love,
the leisurely burn of a million frustrations,
I-know-my-rights in bantam chorale,
the return of the prodigal or the oil-smeared cat.

Accord, boredom, defiance
will turn about their woozy poles.
A far part of the planet will cough up
a new species or relict of an age
fallen long since down the back of memory—

and you will no longer be in the thick
with a shake of the head or *fancy-that* goggle,
no longer start at a forgotten refund
or hear once again after months and months
that odd sort-of-squishing in the downpipe.

It always seems that twilight is fittest—
when sun and blue and heartbeat
can leave seemly and abreast

like three friends through the open doors
of a country pub in deep summer.

But it might be the other end.
You might enfold your everything
and let yourself noiselessly out
as brightness bests the municipal lamps
and the first pint rattles off the wagon.

Few if Any

I can find few if any words
as I walk the hour by hour.
A featureless sky
presses light on a cleared horizon.

I pause to adjust my shoulder-bag,
to stare at the grass round my feet.
Old, forever grass:
there long before I came that way,
mapless, shoving at my breath,
always late by someone's somewhere.

But now I let lateness drain through me
to sink beneath the soil
as a water-spill seems
to dry at a morning window
but still lays up its wetness
where summer can't see.

I cry out
but no echo warms my face.
I fettle a thought
but nothing tempts it to memory
or resolve.
Sky and horizon
stay as open, as closed as ever.
I offer a sigh
just long and deep enough
to prove the bounds of my body.
And move on.

By Way of Testament

St Ives, May 2022

1.
Now, for all the sense I make,
you could say that I speak in stars.
The ground seems to peel away from my every step.
Points of the compass
come at me sweetly randomized,
swishing my calves
like a room of low fitments in the dark.

2.
It seems so long
since I was stitched into the world
and flourished lapels for this occasion
or melted my face into sadness
for that bad go…
since I had an eye to each turn-up for the books,
knew which was front and how to brace against it.

3.
There, look, that's one of me back then:
huge yowza grin, fit to explode
like a granular pie
all over the schoolyard air.
This one's much later,
once the world began tuning its shrieks—
after a final meeting post-breakup,
I forget which one,
anyway when the usual ink set itself slowly drying
on brute change. Yes, me there,
sliding off into another endless night
having left my footsteps at home.

Oh, and this one. Me sat on a sun-again,
rain-again bluff, at peace for a good five minutes—
one for the miscellaneous crew
stuck half over each other
where the album's pinched for space.
Well, well…turns out you can love life
but still find from its earliest strokes
that you've been marked out for excessive shade.

4.
That's why now is as lucent
as any cut petal of time—
with those dying beacons in place of words,
each land inebriate under my feet, .
north-or-is-it-west swooping low
in the lee of south-south-east.

5.
Soon enough, perhaps,
my breath will gently strip out
as a too-slender wire
pulls free of importunate workings.
While that happens
I'd love to find a redoubt of poplars
at a lane's end
on a mid-morning that looks the other way
and turn to vapour,
feel myself willowing up to the heavens
as if cupped in an unceasing turn of hands,
the very last ever to touch me.

Quiet in Whitened Space

Come a certain time I may simply stand,
dust off the moment's particulars,
go to sit quiet in whitened space
and be about my salvation—

watched perhaps by thickets
with all my used heartbeats
impressed on their leaves, or by a river
lonely in its flood, or a hamlet's children
swinging by from one high-coloured chore
to the next.

I'll lean against (as it might be) an elm,
so far back I'm all but hooped within it,
lost in the first of summer
with the bulbous drowse of its one wasp
looping round the hours.

With courteous patience
I'll attend to what has been coming
like Christmas. Perhaps there'll be time
to drink what one of my disappeared selves
once thought a cracking tipple,
then watch as the air itself turns liquid
and gingers down through blue, sapphire,
mauve.

Perhaps too I'll see that crowd
they say comes slowly mobbing at the last—
long-haunting faces, shades rippled
as in the light distress of breeze on stream,
maybe even the cats who slipped my care—

maybe even that latch-key kid
who shared my name and who,
just as we were poised for long trousers,
fell in love with a dark autumn morning
and went west in his own way,
silent, unremarked,
to wherever his river wept its end
against an impervious sea.

Goodbye

I want this to be the last I see
of old coats pouring like dredged effects
from the hook in the kitchen alcove.
Acquaintances turning diagonal to the kerb
and making a ten-minute world for two
between frontage and frontage.
The cat splitting an arrow of midges
as it beats around its acre.
A car revving like a chest-beat
when there's nothing up its backside
or hauling on its grille.
A man in the Co-op tapping his beard
and wondering which queue to crack open.
A girl stepping to the pulse of June,
pausing to check hair and blusher
on her way to a boy who's had a think
and rigged up *goodbye* in his eyes.

I want this to be the last I know
of tickets under wipers,
parakeets with options one to five
in their craws, red skies at night,
ice-blades swinging at the heels of summer,
blue lights fleet across midnight windows,
the lone arc of a siren on a closed afternoon
like an inmate stumbling across a moor
with bowl and dipper,
splashing their madness,
outraging the sun.

Desert Island Dusks

Around this time
I'm always at the rocks.
They trade darks and carmines
like elderly pub men
spinning a single newspaper out
at the foot of an afternoon,
pitting wrath against wrath
at each outrage.

Sometimes one rock
burns near enough as orange
as my mother's old Bex Bissell
which disgorged whenever
it clipped the sideboard
or you tried to ease it widdershins
off the edge of the carpet's world.

The palms mop and mow
at their *well I never* whispers.
Some fronds weep,
others drop straight as those dangly strips
that shrouded the cig-breaks
to the rear of Maud's Uptown Style,
where a girlfriend worked as a basin-maid
for all of two days
till she jiggered a neck-pad
as if farewelling a rabbit
and thirty pounds' worth
of beauty-fettling went west.

The sun drops in slow unspeakable silence,
reminding me of myself at Sunday bedtime
when I'd back out of the living-room

but watch my parents watching TV,
breathe in my not-thereness
as their decline thickened over the air.

Now and then a ship befriends the horizon,
its lights like the lamps of elfin miners
making dogged work of parallel seams.
Sometimes it stops—but really doesn't:
just a trick of forever rotation
seeming to give it a breather
while the gears grind through the depths.

Broken across the last of the light
my stick and tee-shirt
could be a soldier that all war
has wormed hollow.
At first I used them as a rescue-flag.
No longer. All I left behind
is still frolicsome round my head.
To go back now
would be to press *was* on *is*,
likeness on likeness,
but find they refuse the mesh
and muddy up my eyes.

Best to stay put, then—
and, yes, pray most of my memories
can run to a glint that cups noontime
or makes like the first star
marking its wave
and arrowing deep for the morning.

Late Day Final

Here, then. The last poem.
A few-score words
before the air agitates a moment
with all the words stood down
and then sleeps.

The weather could be perkier for it,
but since when has any living thing
had a hand to the lever of the skies?
Enough parades have been rained on,
enough plumes have scuttled away
like mopheads upended.

And this is so small:
a fading mind that wonders
how to voice the final go.

Something about a tree?
But trees, the old song says,
are poems already
and wouldn't thank words
for jockeying their grace.

Or that old-school exercise,
a day in the life of a penny?
But something lifts out of that vanished time
and touches now with frost:
back then a day was worth a day,
now a day is a life.

Well...a face, then,
glimpsed once in perhaps a station buffet,
a fleck of radiance

among the hoicked luggage, the grizzling phones…
beauty marking years confetti'd
to that very moment,
defying the years to come,
each with its bell a touch fainter than the last.

That, then…
something about remembered eyes, skin,
fingers at rest on a brow.
That, then…
perhaps in no buffet
but inches away at the top of a hill
when the first of dark hustles creation.
Eyes…hair…a smile
that says yes, I was an instant near paradise
before it shook out its feathers
and blew on by.

2. And Now the Year Looks Up

Even the Hem of Midsummer

At the side of a field
in the middle of nowhere
a man builds.

Already he has two walls up,
which bracket a single stride of winter.
Their tops angle down from stand to crouch.

In time
a back wall joins them.
The man lays a roof on their slant.

It could be for machinery or feed
though there is nothing for miles
and it feels like forever

since an inch of the country was loved.
For a day or so the man leaves the cold
to mortify stone and rib

then reappears
as if from the pit of an unreckoned hour.
He stares a moment

at how his work has broken the flat of the sky,
then slips inside and curls head to knees,
wrapping his arms tight round.

Look at him willing himself not to be
as if lost in a December
with barely a car along all its roads

or stranded at the fag-end of breakfast
as time pushes down a long table
to a mound of colourless grapes.

He might even think himself
the hem of a cancelled midsummer
brushing silent over the roofs of parish halls

where the streamers have stayed
rucked in their boxes, where the dance
has tried and failed to recover its weave.

Kos, it Says

Kos, it says, *July '98.*
They're sideways on a harbour wall
with the long last of the sun
trailing mauve on the inshore waters.

He's in front, her right hand
on his shoulder. Her dress is long,
olive, puckered at the breast. Her sandals
are soles with a fuss of small buckles.

His trainers are black but he has
white socks also, as if the holiday
can't have the sky full on its face
but must nod homeward—

to his gym-kit, perhaps, or
his chorister's rig at the turn of Advent
in, as it might be, a country town
where the echoes of church are modest.

There is a family resemblance
in the red of their necks, daubed
before noon, maybe, left to ripen
in the placid soak of heat.

They are the only people in the world.
Whoever snapped them is long gone
through the shimmer of barks and doorways.
Perhaps she wonders what a husband

would still be like. Perhaps he imagines
the brother or sister gone from his life
before they arrived, getting exquisitely
up his nose, kicking along beside him.

Turn away a moment. Look back,
closer. Their necks are matching
amulets. Her hand at his shoulder
is squeezing the faintest touch more.

August

And now the year looks up,
scents north and starts to think
of slowly turning its head.
Now prophecies whisper themselves
of frost-beard where leaves
have slipped away,
of afternoons nodding to darkness.
The sun is two parts uncertainty
like a singer still just about
holding a tune. As often
as legs are slapped against midges,
so arms are rubbed unthinking,
shirts deemed adequate, just about,
till vacation blush
folds under equinoctial brown.

Time, perhaps, for a project
to set up dead straight
as the air starts to smell
of old attics. A jigsaw
of Judgement Day with as many pieces
as angels cleaving to a pin.
A walk that each morning
throws out another mile of leading-rope.
Losing the weight you ferried
across the longest days,
with a notion of seeing how thin you can get
so you hang loose and ruckled
round the self you once were,
so you slip through bars of shadow
without snagging a thread.
Or maybe just being
as still as a bird at refuge

while the days lose ballast
and bit by bit the sky unremembers
how to throw the stars easy
or pin them just right
so they cry the white of roses
all across a peaceable blue.

B4976

15th October, 1987

Earlier on today, apparently, a woman rang the BBC and said she heard there was a hurricane on the way. Well, if you're watching, don't worry, there isn't!—Michael Fish, BBC Weather.

That night
a tree massed its bones
on my windscreen,
broke its two hundred seasons
across my grille.

It was a wet road
in hard country
with only liverish light around
glinting as from knives
in maleficent fingers.

It was a moment cut loose
from all binds.
First I was plain autumnal,
reaching to stop the radio stations
from backing into each other,
weariness just beginning
to hobble the relish of upcoming food—
then I wasn't.

All I remember now
is the tree's one surviving leaf,
green as a child could dream it
and suckered on the glass,
only to furl past gold to burnt umber
as dawn came effortfully on—

like a moth tricked out of its flame
that still had to wither and broil itself
on my branch-clamoured screen
in the liverish light of hard country.

Advent

Dawn. A hanging-shroud
starts to be a cloak against a door.
Jesus rests his left calf on his knee,
pulls round his sandal, considers the tread.
Deep as ever though gummed here and there
with the leavings of all the unquiet years,
with ribbon-thread from standards raised
by those who hawked his name as curse,
enchantment, something to yell for want of another.

His feet have tamped down a fair spread of the ages.
Now, with the shoots of distant Gethsemane
drawing in the light, it comes to him
that he must try again, walk again,
un-become himself with each step
by an inch of muscle, a ring of bone,
till sandals loose and drop away
to be storm-fogged like casual markers
of graves for twins of the desert,
till robe and singlet fall as pickings enough
for combers and snafflers where the rush-lit streets begin—

till he furls the last of his what and why
and is again a scrap of heartbeat
staring up at a smoke-worked hole,
wrinkling his nose
at the smell of pelt and burden,
taking in the faces of those
he is charged to bewilder—
hoping that this time neither battle nor blood
will rouse at the first twitch of his hand.

Hibernal

Dell House Retreat, Malvern Wells

Far below this room
branches are elbows
fighting to the clearest air.
Distantly, a hill tires of being seen
and takes mist
to its long, extravagant back.
Clouds unpick their weave
as they come at the roll
of the morning.
And the birds fly so low
they could be forever no more
than an inch over heathland,
wings brushing a rain-cleft
or something's
forsaken scavenge of earth.

Angle Shades in Winter

August set this moth aside
and forgot to retrieve it,
being occupied with scoring cloud
on easterly windows,
netting its brace of provinces
in afternoons brittle or dank.

So the weak-eyed days brought it
to the dust around the log store,
where, under a neck of kindling,
it opened and closed its vinegar wings
like hands in uncertain prayer.

We moved it beneath the pittosporum,
a bush perhaps as flummoxed by its name
as the moth was to be stuck in the pink
among the marbling chills,
below the shunt of bull's breath from the flue.

By morning it was gone…cat, vole,
some other brief extravagance of night.
Or maybe the ghost of summer's end,
rising up at last to claim its own,
found nothing but a tickle or so of wind
from wings powder-dry, spanned,
intent on April.

The angle shades is usually seen between late spring and autumn.

49

Bright Stars

The evening falls. They sit, fingers entwined.
Many a year has died since they broke through
the fastness of cold glaze and, passion-blind,
secured that kiss. He tracks the waning blue
as best he can, his vision failing now.
She moves to gift her bones a touch more ease.
United by one thought, they ponder how
they cheated stasis, voyaged on living seas.

Do they regret it? Never. True, they found
that mortal love can play such merry hell
with heart, tongue, forehead. Now and then around
them brute existence wove the old, old spell:
hurt, pride, indifference. Yet here they are,
together still, still happy to be free
of priest, trussed heifer, pious morning star—
abandoned to that Attic potpourri.

She strokes his cheek. He smiles. The twilight spreads.
'Truth…Beauty,' they reflect. And shake their heads.

3. Like a Hometown Glimpsed as a Train Slows

Centra

Kilfinane, Co. Limerick
'Bright, accessible stores throughout the country'—Centra website

The women who work
in the Kilfinane Centra
live mostly on the edge of town
going Ballylanders way
or cutting up to Ardpatrick.

They hope for nothing from the day
save that it should end as it began
with dryish light
a roof
a ring of gas for the carrots
for the mangetout discounted
with the younger ones safe home
the older ones not unhappily married
Himself half-approachable
at least in fits and starts.

I remember
when some of those houses were built
the ones below the Green Bar
below the shrine where Herself
sobs over the palings of Gethsemane.
Twelve I was or thirteen
adrift on the usual summer visit
flecked with brick-dust myself
from the opening bouts with the world.

I watched the houses going up
the bone and muscle of them
here and there
unpurposed nerves of flex
sun and a transistor on the high planks
'Fabulous 208'…

… and perhaps the Centra women
leashed then in a teen elsewhere
till time at last should find them
down among those sockets
and party walls complete
with the fright of children already in the air
a sleek Himself
not quite tipping to fat
and mostly a dote like
save when the roasties were too soon for the plate
or he had the drink taken.

Petrol at Yarnton

Second Saturday in a row for Lance
and the lie-in would have been mint.
But he can't complain. Trisha's mum
has taken another darkward turn
and it's no small step to Burnley.
She's promised to spell him off
the following Thursday, nice of her
but of course she'll sign in as him—
unless Pardoe descends from on high
with his mouth full of the usual non-karma
from Head Office, yellow-card oaths
about messing up the rota—in which case
she'll say, ooh, thing is, Lance, he's proper poorly
but my mother's hanging in there, Mr Pardoe,
thought you'd like to know.

Six am. Radio Oxford gives over
with the fol-de-rol about sofa bonanzas
and the latest fly-by-nights who'll buy any car
with that double-speed voice troughing
on terms and conditions,
and it's onto the news at the top of the hour,
the bonny bunch of frights from round the world.
Lance rolls up the metal cover
to let the army of vaping tools blink and breathe,
regards the bucket of three-for-one choc surprises,
thinks to check their sell-by date, must've been there
since Valentine's easy, forgets, smooths the strips
of lucky-dip tickets in their scuffed plastic case,
tells himself he must buy one right now, he did all right
with those HotPicks a month back,
forgets again because here's pump two already pinging—

Bertie Burrows with his van full of roses
heading for Blenheim, some big do on there, apparently.
So...Bertie's given in again. Always complaining
that what they pay wouldn't keep him
in bumper-bolts, says each time will be the last,
but he's sweet on one of the under-gardeners,
Czech girl, or is it Latvian, so he probably reckons
thin margins are worth it for a floribunda smile
from easterly Europe. Now pump three, pump five—
caravan-civilians on a getaway, towing the weekend
eight-wheeled behind them. Lance settles up with Bertie,
suffers his 'Bloody Blenheim, Lance my friend,
never again', remembers the choc-surprise bucket,
decides to move it to the window, well,
weather's meant to stay cool, they won't goo up,
forgets again because here's one of the caravanners
asking the best way to Witney, you'd think
with their hoedown of whistles and bells
they could pack a satnav but seemingly not.

Radio Oxford's interviewing someone
who's made a replica of something
out of something you wouldn't think
you could make something with. Lance
asks the caravanner if his interest
would run to a choc surprise or two,
for the kids, like (well, it'd lighten the bucket,
and now he comes to think of it,
haven't they been there since Christmas?). But no dice.

And now the lads at the car-wash down the way
are lining up their sponges and unspooling
the hoses from the wall. Turkish, Trisha
reckons, or Greek, fair play to them,
work the full canteen of hours—

54

give Bertie the occasional slosh-down
free, gratis and for nowt. Or maybe he pays them
in roses, which they gingerly cellophane after
and dispatch to, dunno, some black-aproned grandma
in Antalya or Crete. Someone bedevilled by distance and tears.

Pump five, eight, three, one…the hop-to-it pulses
bounce all over the screen. Then the seasoned tizzy
of cash and cards (and someone goes for a fist
of choc surprises…result). Then quiet for all of five minutes
save the hoosh and dwindle along the Oxford road
and some oik fingering the water-can by pump five—
Lance ready to rap the window—before he slopes off
with his head full of gunk. Then pump two.
And there's Bertie driving back again, must have made
a smart delivery, or maybe he finally thought, stuff Blenheim,
I'll shift the lot on St Giles's before the coppers infringe.
Or maybe that under-gardener withheld her Czech-Latvian smile
and sent him, poor bugger, back into the world
with his heart as cold as the wind
that's just getting up and giving the signage what for.

The Orphans of Midsomer

Midsomer Murders, ITV, 1997 onwards

And every so often
a young person stares unseeing
over and around the last five minutes.
The Inspector pats their shoulder,
the DS gives a smile his heart
can't really afford, because already the next case
is among the foliage, the credits are antsy
at the foot of the screen. Doors must slam.
The unmarked car must drive
into this time next week.

So the young person
without so much as a neighbourly hug
is left to stand outside what they're stuck with:
a cottage in which the odours have to stoop,
a mansion where the chill huddles into itself
at corniced junctions—
Death's pay in kind, there being no other family,
not truly, mum or dad having hooked it
before the episode began,
the other one having been fed to the plot,
even unmasked as the murderer
brewing more grudges than all the hot dinners
touted in the breaks.

A proper wrong 'un
will always fight the glove
that seeks to pilot their head
through the squad-car's rear door.
So it is now, before the orphan's unmendable heart.

The DS and Inspector
will make off through ending's dusk,
fade in step with their tail-plate.
The supporting cast will tumble
into the run-off down the sides of the script.
Only the orphan remains and is real,
standing before a house whose secrets
will never now stop yakking.
Maybe they'll pray for their own tomorrow
(though veiled as yet by that fight of names,
key grip, location bod, gaffer…)—
even tell themselves they can almost see it,
like a hometown glimpsed as a train slows,
half-melted in an indifference of rain.

4. Rocking Horse Dreams

Sugar-shake and 'Meg

Ross Point, Grenada, August 1995

We sit beneath the awning of Fortreau's coffee stop,
watch the rain as it mulches the harbour.
Big changes coming. Esp and Twinko
go be cruise troubadours, plying ritzily
way over to the Keys. Scholarship Mitchell
is set to booglarise Berlin. For me, Canada,
a Maritime campus with Yule-card snow,
however that turns out to feel.

Esp putzes around with the wrappers of sugar-shake.
I think of our forefathers, our foremothers
in their mist. Sugar braided them in iron,
drew them here from Benin, from the brushtracks
of Côte d'Ivoire, the Niger's delta claws below Asaba.
Worked them till the cane did fail,
till the ledgers caught an everlasting colic—
then, only then, turned them loose as fire ants
evaluating skin at a beach fete.

Twinko is all animation concerning his buccaneer gig,
scoops the torn wrappers, rolls them to a tight little ball.
Now I'm minded of nutmeg, sugar's inheritor
two hundred years gone, salvation of all the milords—
how it brought to the island Madeiran songs,
Maltese oaths, the solemnities of Asia.
How it guided those new hands to rattle it
from the branches, to split off the mace from the 'meg.

Indentured, all them, which sort of means slaved
except you get a collar to your shirt.

Our forebears didn't want that arseness—
did go instead to farm plots,
ship what the seasons permitted
to the Grenadines and beyond.
Some years the seeds wouldn't budge.
Some dawns the boats went down
within spit of Mayreau or Canouan.

Ah sah, what blessing could speak for them?
Sheath-rot freed them, not remorseful hearts.
And now it have us four about our casting-off,
throwing our own shapes in fortune's bacchanal.
Mitchell flicks the 'meg ball high into the cloud.
I try hard not to think what that might mean.

Fancy Min

Harford Village, St Andrew Parish, Grenada

All Fancy Min ever wanted, she said,
was to fall face down and movie-trick slow
in the white of a northern winter,
then do the up-down arm-drag thing,
fashion herself an angel, which would rise
and sheathe her heart between its wings.

One of old Dom Colcaxo's girls,
the eldest of six but the youngest,
inheritor of his rocking-horse dreams,
the way he'd be forever about to become,
the way he'd sculpt and patch
his pristine live-long nothings.

Min the doomed date-fool,
head fit to sunder with images
from a breakneck skim of all the glossies
let slip by the witching sky:
Marilyn, Lana, a passel of Jodies and Jaynes,
Naomi Campbell, too, Whoopi, Oprah…

favourable ballast for all us, those last,
who had the same long-invisible skin,
someway the same curve of muscle.
But ah sah, each date a Passchendaele,
with her dragging back to Colcaxo place
at dawn, mud-eyed, heels half-broke.

Till one night it have flashing lamps
and whips of commotion, and Min
gingered up their path to the howl

of the village-end pot hounds,
and she dying, my mother revealed,
about the time the sun scratches and stirs.

Some ba-john out of St George's harbour-holes
or tourist, maybe, with a belly overhang,
who couldn't turn a single head in Manchester
or Brooklyn but was royal drunk and crazy,
full of what-happens-here-stays-put. Whoever,
some plane hooshed his malfeasance clean away.

Colcaxo moved his crew off-island,
Trinidad, my father said, San Fernando East.
At long last tangled with a tap of work,
breaking stone where creeper song
scissors the noon. Like each downswing
go bust the ba-john's head.
Like the rubble go monumentalise
and beam on out to the raggedest cloud
with Min's face,
her child-woman smile,
her heels unbusted.

Pot hound: a stray, hungry dog.

Ba-john: a bully, a tough customer.

5. I'm Not in Control. I'll Never be Safe.

Safe

1.
I could live
in a rectory
with its own deep silent ground
by the bus stop and common grass
of a stone village
away from the fat of the city
the serrated cough of the town.
A village where people were pleasant
but had no call to know me
save perhaps an elderly couple
who took a shine
because I perhaps reminded them
of a son now lost
to the hard light of the uplands.
A couple who would show me the ropes
and in return be content
with a modest interest only
in their kitchen garden
their charcoals of the local views
and the birds of Michaelmas.

2.
Pray God another night
in a far part of the rectory
where the brickwork
smuggles comfort in
while pretending the cold of iron.
Pray God
another night

unspoken to
undemanded
unrequired
unfound.

3.
The housekeeper's ruddiness
precedes her into the kitchen
is as round and wide
as the belly of the stove
we take it in turns to feed.
It's good of her to stay on
but as she says
why wouldn't she?
everyone's gone
from her life too
save a husband
whom she calls the dad
a figure given to long
motionless stares
who says that rain
makes the world taller
and sets elegant little fires
in secluded places
to keep it from the chills.

4.
The wife
of the elderly kind couple
sometimes follows the dad
to where he occasions
a new fire.
If a spark
were to jump his shoulder
and ignite her

she says
pouring the tea
she wouldn't mind.
The world
she says
has often enough walked
back and forth
through her and hubby
and never not forgotten
to wipe its feet
even sometimes made a virtue
of unhinging their gate onto the lane.
She'd love
she says
to burst into a rare bloom
of dispatching flame
and at the thought of it
the years fall away from her giggle
as if it were her girlhood self
running past the window
late for time
and not caring tuppence.

5.
Now and then a boy comes round
from the pepper of new houses
at the village end.
No harm in him says the housekeeper
just dozy as the day
nine she reckons maybe ten
running a touch to fat
frown-strokes at the bridge of his nose
working in for the duration.
His class at the primary school
have been learning about castles

encouraged to seek one out.
For him the rectory
is a hamper of echoes
a run of wood doing odd things
where the stairs turn
an obliging sigh from the long-ago
when he stamps a foot in the hallway
and so is castle enough.
The housekeeper lets him in
and he stays until he goes.
Sometimes I see him
along the gallery landing
gazing on the portrait
of a gone incumbent
nose-wings pinched
with seeming rectitude—
or loitering at the study door
as if to fling in
with news as grey as lovelessness.
Each time he leaves
he stops a moment in the porch
presses a hand to the grouting
and murmurs
My liege, the men are fitly disposed.

6.
By way of chat
the housekeeper asks
if I know how long I'll be staying.
I don't answer straight off.
I'm tied to nothing save time
whose features at last
are here and there clearer to me
who now walks an inner path
parallel with mine.

To be going on with
the elderly kind couple
have invited me for Christmas
have asked me
to be their son for a bit
though I doubt either one
has thought it aloud.
Still I wouldn't be surprised
to find myself in his room
breathing his triumphs
in the still of Christmas Eve
gazing at all his trophies
like a raggedy pilgrim
before I switch off the light.

I smile at the housekeeper
turn her question round and round
as if it's the cup I'm drying.
No definite plans
I tell her
see how it goes into the new year
and saying that
I'm a child again
younger than the pudgy boy
with his castle dreams and his lurking
I'm as bright again as a holiday start
and all undamaged.

'The new year'—
a lake of a phrase
a sea shrugging off its horizon
where I can scull
between hospitable nowheres
look up at a blue
where all is unbegun.

The new year—
outflowing the inky strictures
of hour and week
never asking
that I do or be a single thing
at any point
in all its immeasurable reaches.

I stand with my fingertips
half among cloth
half on the cold of the china.
On its inner path
time still paces me
but I sense now a brief reluctance
as if it would rather leave me alone
step off and save its bones
would rather look up at whatever
its own secret blue might be.

7.
We're due snow
and it could be heavy.
According to the dad
snow makes the world
even taller than rain
pushes it clear
to the spaces where
the used-up stars huddle
the discarded silences cohere
in the kind of afterwards
that might follow
someone's unwise admission
or a verdict in a thoughtless rush
or the word of war.

Whether or not the snow comes
the world
says the dad
will need cheer about its nethers
and so it is that for Christmas night
he has planned another fire
that is none of the parish council's concern
this time between a forest's edge
and a comma of outlying trees.

The castle kid will be there
the elderly kind couple
a friend of the dad's from army days
who is buckled tight into himself
I hear
who moves between charity feeds
and the broader sort of doorway—
he and the housekeeper
will do something by way of a thermos
a bottle
a put-aside cake
for us to have as the fire wakes
as its yellows and ambers
release the dark from its joylessness
as we gaze up and along the trees
till we find the roof of the year.

Beyond the fire
the living stars will wait
to shine on all the coming
wheres and whens
on the kind of human joy that will try
to hoodwink the stony tracts
the kind of love that will seek

to take full breath
and not disappear unknown.

8.
Afterwards
back at the kind couple's house
as we wait
for the castle kid's mother to arrive
he drops out of the steady talk
to ask in a low voice
if I believe in the cavalry.

The question surprises me
saddens
that he should so young
have come to know that need
then again
how much older was I
when it found me?

Always
I tell him
always I believe
and I let a smile stand in
for further explanation:
that delay and misreading
can prey as devoutly on the cavalry
on those who would rescue
as on a stranger
with a first foot
to the earth of a new beginning—
that my rescuers always found
the right place
but also and as often
that I'd done with my weltering there

had moved myself on
to the echo of sobbing and terrible words
that I'd fumbled up some new arrangement
which would do for a bit
which was held together as often as not
by filament and gum
by peace that lasted a taper's length.

Always
my smile does not tell the kid
my cavalry and I have been
a goodish day's ride adrift.

But those were my years.
Who's to say he won't
some or most times
find salvation or at least reprieve
on something like the dot?
Or that I shan't
even now
just the once
a little way along from here
or further
when as it might be the stars have burned low
and the zenith is as blank
as a dawn that refuses its onset?

Slowly the castle kid
returns my smile
again the steady talk finds us
and all around the kitchen walls
the fire plays its bright and changeful hand.

6. The Scarps and Highways

Quickened

Fresh in from elsewhere
a blackbird lands on a branch,
another sky on its wings
and, sealed still in its eyes,
the slow commotion of daybreak
as it pieced itself together.

It stalks along and back,
grubbing at time as it pulses,
till someone in a kitchen
catches sight and says
to their vine-graven tiles,
to the sink on which
their cold hands are pressing,
Oh, look…

then slips it into a pocket at their heart—
that moment when a blackbird
scattered all vacancy,
dipped to a skittish leaf
and quickened the indifferent light
around where all at once it wasn't.

...another...another...

All at once a bird sings
somewhere above the back gate
to the lane behind the houses.
Its morning moment
laces up the world:
children behind
half-drawn curtains
wrestling with sums;
a man in line
at a service station
numbed of a sudden
by bewilderment
at what he's doing
and why he was born;
a woman sipping her coffee
while eyeing her suitcase
at the foot of the stairs;
a couple touching hands
for the first time in ages;
a cat nosing over its final meal,
a squirrel branch-hanging
just a swipe away from a feeder.
A birth...a birth...another...another...
a crocodile of torches
lit in sequence down a darkened pass.

Yes

A blackbird stands on a branch
above where philadelphus
makes the path feel less alone.
It's the moment when day
starts threading down hand over hand,
stuck about with the odd small glory.

The bird sings the whole mad run of the world
to the second it opened its beak.
War and pleasure bubble in its notes.
Late rain clicks at the greenhouse
as though an irradiated man hides there
and the elements baulk at his wormy blood.

And now a plastic bag
cartwheels past the gate to the lane.
The blackbird sees off its tale of the hour just gone
and flies. Imagine them rising together
wet with the first tears of night,
making for what doesn't know it will be dawn.

Imagine the bird dropping notes into the bag
like unstrung pearls with no floor for their skitter.
Imagine the bag as a singing moon…
…till they swerve apart,
the bird to rise on,
the bag to cascade the knockings of a song

that someone might assemble as they wear against the dark
and try through once or twice…and find
a yes, small and improbable, itching at their heart.

Jenga

Not a four walls enthusiast.
His were the scarps and highways
of the garden,
the shrubs above him
high as Nordic pines.
Mid-morning by the summer-house
he'd turn from whatever labours
the cat-world confects
and just sit,
then maybe take on a fence-post
or have an unavailing lick
at one of his off-white paws.

Jem, I called him for a bit,
but mostly we settled for Jen.
Jenga was thrown round him
like a kid's brute embrace
by whoever had him before he arrived,
an RSPCA two-for-one
with a sister who died years ago.
To begin with he stayed a good seven days
in the sideboard's under-shadow,
fearing the rough-house would simply resume
in this new, just as frightening land.

The evening after his sister died
he patrolled the living room
chair by chair and cover by cover,
sensing that the world now nursed
a black-and-white-shaped absence.
Before much longer
our lonely tabby might search the same,
still hearing in her own way

his morefoodnow plaint.
And maybe she'll wait in a room's open country
for the off-white clip round her ear
which he'd deliver at full-bowl time,
and which, in the ether behind her eyes,
he may keep on doling without a care
from whatever pocket Eden
now protects him.

7. Seven Unanchored

An Open Square

The taxi's not due till eleven.
I finish my coffee, look about.
Already the house is lessening,
paring its light as if to get
the jump on me. Chairs and counters
hang between solid touch and hands through.
Doors work back to virgin grain.
Photographs slowly round up
all those smiles, unfeature
the throw of seasons behind them.
Even next door's cat, snouting the privet
on its eternal beat, turns from tabby
to mist, whorls of greenleaf
strung within its fur.

Now the telephone distils to missed calls,
all that hurt and vexation fogging the dial.
Upstairs, something softly thuds:
the first width or depth
easing free of the high dimensions.
The windows sigh.
Soon they'll have no irresolute shadows
to put before the world.
Soon the taxi-driver will have no need
to hunt or check—
will come upon me in an open square,
where a history is done
with its little perturbations
and strews itself in dust-runes
at my feet.

A Fuss of Keys

The man is slow along the street
between the corner
and where the first cars are parking
for the day. Now and then he stops
as if he were caught in tropic space
and his years were tree-thrown bars of sun
that must secure their right levels
all down him. A fuss of keys
dances at his belt-loop:
tiny metal maps
for the car he must find,
the home that lies
in the eye of revs and motion—
perhaps a key too for a shed
in which he will gingerly chamfer time
till, called in for the night's meal,
he takes a last look at whatever he's fashioned
and reckons it will do to be going on with,
will bear the weight of diffident prinking
as tomorrow gets itself up on its wall,
stares about, drums heels
at pace with its catchless breath.

Spinning Out

She sees but doesn't
as she spins her coffee out.
Behind her, morning squishes wide
against the station buffet.
Train liveries drape across their line of travel,
suffer the shunt and wheeze of doors
and half-tumbled bodies.
Flecks of coat, profiles, case-wheels
play into the platform's rolling wave.

Beside her a jackpot machine
works through its scraggly repertoire
of come-hither tunes. A silver-hinged case
with man attached wallows up at a nearby table.
She tilts her cup higher.
The man asks if she's finished with the paper
she hasn't read. She twitches *be my guest.*
Her eyes don't move.

She's off to meet
a maybe beau coughed up on the web.
She has to be at an upstairs conference room
full of tumblers and iffy pens
where arterial roads meet wisps of country.
She's spending time with a uni daughter
caught on the spikes between childhood and all to come.
She's visiting mum and dad as per norm
or after an estrangement that began
when someone said or didn't say
in some lost, time-shrouded moment.
There's no local bed available—the best they can do
is a clinic she can't picture
far over a hill of strange parishes.

The silver-hinged case hauls its man away.
He drops the paper in front of her
with half a thanks. Her eyes don't move.
She finishes her coffee. Of a sudden
she checks her watch, pats her pockets
as if she'd forgotten she was with herself,
re-fusses the scarf at her throat
to stymie the world's consternation.
Arranges herself round her deepest breath.
Leaves to the sound of a ringtone
trilling *Someone To Watch Over Me.*

Throatline

A man walks down the last street
of the old year. The throatline of his shoes
cups tight round his instep—like that doctor's hands
half a century ago, dimly remembered
at some or other faff
to do with posture.

His tread remembers
crisper vamps of roughout,
big-hearted canvas quarters,
how they curated steps
easier and faster
round worlds drawn up for him,
worlds he patched himself—
playground, thorn-track, mezzanine,
solemnly mountable stairs
topped with a waiting scroll
or a priest's echo-whipping cough
(when he dropped his ring for her
so it bounced off the welt
of those mirror-blacks:
they spent two years
trying not to understand the note it sang
but it never shook them free.
He still has his, though,
in the shadows and folds piled woozy
at the far end of the loft).

There was that time
upper and shank divorced
at the head of a platform
so he missed the train
and the job and its life

went to someone
with yessir brogues.
But that other time too
with its many relations
when he kicked all lazy
at the top of an afternoon
in those cod-baseball boots
('None genuine without this trim')
whose toebox was guaranteed
to unfirm itself after weeks
of hike and slide and drum-pedal.

Now the year drops away.
The truth of age
flowers cold through his backstays
and snugs along his tongues.
He will not need another pair.

Like the First Bird

A man gets off a train in a town he doesn't know.
Already others are pulling their mornings
around them. Light hollows channels
for first footsteps, the drag of crates
to hold shop doors ajar. Greetings are tuned
as to that very moment a week ago,
crossing beeps haunt their little green men
on the usual frozen jog.

Miles back,
the man left his history handkerchief-neat
in the buffet-car, alongside a sandwich
with more than the usual fight.
Now he makes first use of himself,
stares with birthday eyes
at bellied awnings, a parked van
letting its indicators goof,
a group, small, anxious, elderly
beneath a sign for recycling.

Soon he might lose himself in wonder
at the tumbling heart of a moment
and try big things like buying a paper
or looking for a street
whose name he hears on the ripening air
and likes the sound of. Or perhaps
he'll stop a body and tell them
such bits of his name as he remembers,
ask how they go about expanding
till they touch the sides of each hour.

The man thinks
of someone uncovering all he was
where he tucked it against the leavings of bread—
and helplessly laying off what they were
to become what they can't yet know.
And hopes that, even so,
they'll by and by swing down into the day
as to a child with open gaze
who spreads hands and says,
forget all that…just look…just look.

The Man with no Umbrella

The man with no umbrella
lives with a raindrop in his ear
it gossips of tides and oceans
how the dogdays
would see it mist out of the waves
how it would find them again
at the dark swing of the weatherglass

its earliest memory it insists
is of waking to itself
amongst the toils of Eden
binding with the millions
to pour down on Adam and Eve
marry them fast to their guilty clothes
so hard
the sword of the sentinel-angel
rusted like prayer

it crawled it says
into and out of the bitten apple
which tasted of a colour
you wouldn't wish to dream

over time it has mimicked
a tear on a cheek
and so sealed misunderstandings—
where kindred pairs have parted
hidden in separate footsteps
while the ill-sorted have pushed on
working their lips

for this the raindrop is sorry

the man understands but just stares down
he has lived so long
he has nothing of his own to hear
if he thinks at all
it's of the umbrellas
he's left among the years
the trains they might still be riding
the music that might still be stuck
among their folds
with the click of last lights
the long gasp of dark across a stage

it was bad admits the raindrop
but not bad bad
just that the dove overshot Noah's prow
so the millions had to bulk a last squall
to turn it back

of course
it might have been making
for a land of birds elsewhere
happy to let the ark turn
to a drifting bonescape

in which case says the raindrop
I wouldn't be here
feeling the smoke of your mind
you wouldn't be picturing where you are not
as it fills up with umbrellas

the man hears this and doesn't
he is looking at a long-ago summer afternoon
a Friday with time caught between strikes
four-fifty four-fifty-five
a campus and everyone gone

departure tugging hard at the world
the world digging in like a mule

he stands in an adjacent park
the campus gate he came out of
will stay bang shut
till an autumn he won't be in
all that quitting smells heavy as musk
as a raindrop rolls off a leaf
another and another
waking him for the first time
to his open throat
thin collar
empty hands

The Going Light

Wigginton, Hertfordshire, June 2021

Even now,
after all that's faltered
and left promises half-buzzed,
summer can still burst out of my eyes
and I can find the going light
through the mudlands,
across the floes of yesterday's desire.

Sometimes my body
can recover its stockinged height
and meet the morning easy on the nose.

Of course the shadows breed
and menace the fattest candle,
rattle like lengths unbolted,
go up and over like gallows-hoods,
close like the hands of assassins.

But even so a day can break
at beautifully goonish angles
to grant me a dogleg of June skies,
a lazy brush of warmth
as from leaves grown broad
in unimpeded places,
webbed and coloured
exactly as a child would dream them.

8. Fastnesses

Ways to Say It

Footsteps go down the stairs.
A door closes. After that,
the silence is deeper
than the drop from that clutter-shelf
to the tiles that share a crack
like a sealed mouth. Strange
how such sounds can work together,
contriving pocket finales:
the castanetting of curtain-hoops,
the far detonation
of a stuck drawer nearly shut.
Sometimes it seems
that a house knows goodbye
before any other word
and slowly brims with all those ways
to say it—letting them slip
like something off a mantelpiece
on a morning when the world
is shod in felt. A postcard
from a season that's lost its light.
A docket for some passing service,
costed by a spider. A note,
folded just the once,
saying don't ever try to find me.

Old-school

Empty now,
the bottle of old-school aftershave
has survived each lunging cull
and lives at the back of the cabinet
beneath the bathroom sink.
Alongside is a horse-hair brush
with a base of winter-chapped red
like a tiny buoy hauled ashore
from a childhood sea.
A bowl, too, of medicated soap,
Measham's or Daunt's,
scarped and abraded
to an old-gold moon
like the broached lid
of a miniature Party Four.

They share a quiet
such as is found beneath leaves
when light falls back
and the climb of the earliest owl
threads thicket to star. History too—
days long gone under the main
when Fridays after mealtime
meant ritual, sluiced armpits,
faces confected brow to jaw
in mirrors angled to catch
each nip of skin and, just behind,
a bathroom wall's posy of oceanic fronds.

Hope was there as well,
winking at the mirror's edge,
promising low murmurs
at a table where the other lads weren't,

a coat gallantly unfolded
for slim arms to snug on,
a homeward walk to a gate
with parental watchfulness
globed in an outside light—
promising arrangements for the next time
if luck played nice,
then all the times after,
tiny steps through the big who-knows
as if it were a book of shapes
that reserves the right to pick its own colours—
high-day white, blaring yellow,
maybe at the end the deep gentle orange
of all to be looked back on
in modest happiness, feasible calm.

Party Four: a large can of Watneys Bitter beer, first launched in 1964.

Ruckled

The cover was ruckled
on the far side of the bed
from my sitting there
to rub morning into my feet.
I forgot to straighten it
when I stood up and became yet again
a creature which the day
might pick up and study.

So the ruckles lived a while
as whitecaps
while hour fell against hour—
whispered among themselves,
hoped to evade the incontinent sun,
traded memories of throws
and car-rugs they'd passingly sculpted…

paused only when shadows
flung and busied up the stairs,
wondering if I or somebody else
would come barrelling in
near-intemperate with order
and undo them with a planing hand…

not that they would die—
ruckles are never smoothed
but pulse away like fish
beneath house-beautiful streams
till they find commodious elsewheres
in which to flag themselves up
and revive their unknowable joy
at fizzing the angle, singing the line
to sleep.

Courtroom Artist

They are seated under my pen.
The ways in which
they have shaded a bruise
around the blush of life
or themselves become one
must be caught in the time it takes
for the press-room to swell
and disgorge.
My notes ahead of the sketches
are pins in butterflies.
Goo goo cheeks
becomes the rotundity
of a man who killed a town.
Eight-balls are the razored heads
of boys hauled up for night-racing
on the lawless sweeps
round carriage-lamp estates
or coining it as mules
for solubles among the languid classes.
Bone-cage, on the other hand,
assembles the proper bearing
of a woman who never slipped up in her life
save when she turned away
that one particular moment
and ghost fingers prised her from herself,
parlaying money and breath and name
into pickings to be couriered
through the dark air
of a world you'd never catch existing.

All of Time

One is from a sleepier part of the Sixties,
has a raised face with a proper wood surround
which the maker has spared the hurt of starbursts.
It ticks like a mannerly gent with no paper to hand,
obliged to whisper a secret over and over;
chimes the nine and twelve only,
in a roll of pulses without a tip.

The other is from any time in the last thirty years
and has known the pit of a trolley-case,
shared a rolled sock with unspent cash. Small, it is,
black-bodied. Nothing before it was ever truly square.
Instead of a tick it is a mower beyond a faraway hill,
idling. Its alarm is a peewit trying not to be.

They live in a side room no-one uses much,
the first on an unabused mantel, the other
on an old mad bookcase with split shelves
that just miss each other's height. Nobody
looks in at them, though the first is wound,
the other fed batteries at need. The first
is five minutes behind. Only fair—
it has lived longer, has the right
to let the other comfort an old year at its drop
and scout out the puzzle of the new,
to happen lazily on some zero-hour crisis,
dinky and noisy beneath that roof.

Between them they are all of time,
send it out to live and die and live
on the unheated air between their faces,
to slice and bevel the lives adjacent,
make like a gout of lead or the brush of an open coat

dashing from platform to platform.
Soon enough will come the last slam
of a door. Time will speed the house to rafter-bones
to lock-up to shelter to sand. The clocks themselves
will be glints and hands only, adrift in what's to come.
Still they'll keep the faith. Moons will rise
to the mannerly whispers of a secret,
the two-tone of a peewit trying not to be.

Fastness

I can't remember much
before moving into this poem.
Bits of early school, where the same clock
followed me from room to room
and giants with artillery mouths
and clouds on their shoulders
broke off pieces of the sky
and threw them at faraway heads.
Come teenage years I was entrusted
with creating horrors for myself.
After that life starved and sated by turn,
riotous Edens trading off
with the sounds of a house
that has seen its last departure—
a drip from the bathroom
irking the stairs,
a choked pipe's last furl of cold.

This poem measures a mile
by a mile. Its images are smooth-ish
and happily fit most pockets.
None of it droops head to hand
or has sex with primeval words.
Sometimes at evening
I walk its bounds,
now a boast of thickets,
now a view of the downlands
I must have outrun to get here.
On occasion, when the wind tires
and stillness makes things taller,
I hear and see tiny play-acts
out of what I lived before:
a sighing refusal,

thumbprint insistences,
voices turning aside in the dusk...
and ever and again a hand rising
to squeeze my age-narrowed arm
and somebody saying, never mind,
you're alright, you, you're alright.

Acknowledgements

The author and publishers gratefully acknowledge the magazines in which the following poems have appeared:

'A boy looks out', *Poetry Salzburg Review* 38, Spring 2022
'Uffern gwaedlyd', *Dream Catcher* 47, Summer 2023
'Deeper in, further off', *Under the Radar* 29, Autumn 2022
'Slow to clear', *The Cannon's Mouth* 84, June 2022
'That lane gone by', *Whispering Dialogue*, volume 16, January 2022
'Thursdays', *Poetry Salzburg Review* 38, Spring 2022
'From this day', *Sarasvati* 066, September-November 2022
'Sins beyond its making', *Whispering Dialogue*, volume 17, April 2022
'Last and closest', *The Journal* 64, Autumn 2021
'Goodbye', *Under the Radar* 29, Autumn 2022
'Even the hem of midsummer', *Critical Survey*, volume 33, issue 3-4, September 2021
'Kos, it says', featured in 'Imagined Histories: poetry Q&A with Alison Chisholm', *Writing Magazine*, October 2021
'August', *Dream Catcher* 47, Summer 2023
'Advent', *Dream Catcher* 39, 2019
'Angle shades in winter', *Wet Grain* 2, Summer 2021
'Bright stars', *Sarasvati* 066, September-November 2022
'The Orphans of Midsomer', *The Cannon's Mouth* 84, June 2022
'Fancy Min', *Pennine Platform* 88, 2020
'Quickened', *Pennine Platform* 88, 2020
'Yes', *Obsessed With Pipework* 99, August 2022
'An open square', *The Cannon's Mouth* 84, June 2022
'Spinning out', *Ink, Sweat and Tears* [online], June 2023
'Throatline', *Pennine Platform* 90, 2021
'Like the first bird', *London Grip New Poetry* [online], Autumn 2022
'The going light', *Sarasvati* 066, September-November 2022
'Ways to say it', *The Cannon's Mouth* 84, June 2022

'Old-school', featured in 'A Scent of the Past: poetry Q&A with Alison Chisholm,' *Writing Magazine*, March 2023
'Fastness', *Sarasvati* 066, September-November 2022

'Centra' was Highly Commended in the Charles Causley International Poetry Competition, 2020.

'Ruckled' was long-listed in the Poetry Society's National Poetry Competition, 2022.

About the Author

Michael W. Thomas has published nine collections of poetry, three novels and two collections of short fiction. His most recent poetry collection, prior to this, is *Under Smoky Light* (Offa's Press); his most recent short fiction collection is *Sing Ho! Stout Cortez: Novellas and Stories* (Black Pear Press); his most recent novel is *The Erkeley Shadows* (KDP / Swan Village Reporter). With Simon Fletcher, he edited *The Poetry of Worcestershire* (Offa's Press). His work has appeared in *The Antigonish Review* (Canada), *The Antioch Review* (US), *Critical Survey, Crossroads* (Poland), *Dream Catcher, Etchings* (Australia), *Irish Studies Review, Irish University Review, Magazine Six* (US), *Pennine Platform, Poetry Salzburg Review, The Times Literary Supplement* and *Under the Radar,* among others. He has reviewed for *The International Journal of Welsh Writing in English, London Magazine, Other Poetry* and *The Times Literary Supplement,* and is on the editorial board of *Crossroads: A Journal of English Studies* (University of Bialystok, Poland). He was long-listed for the National Poetry Competition, 2020 and 2022, and long-listed and short-listed for the Indigo Dreams Spring Poetry Prize, 2023. For more information, please visit:
www.michaelwthomas.co.uk
Additionally, Michael has a blog, *The Swan Village Reporter:*
http://swansreport.blogspot.com/